Langston Hughes

Philip S. Bryant

Raintree

Chicago, Illinois

© 2003 Raintree
Published by Raintree, a division of Reed Elsevier, Inc.
Chicago, Illinois
Customer Service 888-363-4266
Visit our website at www.raintreelibrary.com

For information, address the publisher
Raintree, 100 N. LaSalle, Suite 1200, Chicago, IL 60602

Printed and bound in the Unites States at Lake Book Manufacturing, Inc.
07 06 05
10 9 8 7 6 5 4 3

Library of Congress Cataloging-in-Publication Data:

Bryant, Philip S.
  Langston Hughes / Philip S. Bryant.
      p. cm. -- (African American biographies)
Summary: Profiles African American writer Langston Hughes, who worked to promote a better understanding of people of different racial, religious and cultural backgrounds through his poetry and lectures.
Includes bibliographical references and index.
  ISBN 0-7398-6871-3 (HC), 1-4109-0037-1 (Pbk.)
  1. Hughes, Langston, 1902-1967--Juvenile literature. 2. Poets, American--20th century--Biography--Juvenile literature. 3. African American poets--Biography--Juvenile literature. [1. Hughes, Langston, 1902-1967. 2. Poets. 3. African Americans--Biography.] I. Title. II. Series: African American biographies (Chicago, Ill.)

PS3515.U274Z6175 2003
818'.5209--dc21

2002153360

Acknowledgments
The publishers would like to thank the following for permission to reproduce photographs:
pp. 4, 14, 48 Hulton/Archive by Getty Images; pp. 8, 10, 17, 38, 46, 51 CORBIS; pp. 12, 21, 26, 32, 33, 34, 43, 53, 57 Bettmann/CORBIS; pp. 22, 25 National Portrait Gallery, Smithsonian Institution/Art Resource, NY; p. 29 The Mariners' Museum/CORBIS; pp. 30, 41 Underwood & Underwood/CORBIS; p. 45 Scheufler Collection/CORBIS; p. 54 Ted Williams/CORBIS; p. 58 Ralf-Finn Hestoft/CORBIS.

Cover photograph: Bettmann/CORBIS

Content Consultant
Dr. Paul Reuben
Department of English
CSU Stanislaus

Some words are shown in bold, **like this.** You can find out what they mean by looking in the Glossary.

Contents

Langston Hughes wrote poems, plays, and prose that have been an inspiration for many great African-American artists. It has only been since his death that his work has gained the recognition his supporters always believed it deserved.

Introduction

Langston Hughes is one of the most important American poets of the twentieth century. He was among the first African-American writers to see the poetry in everyday black speech and to use it in his own writing. He celebrated the beauty not only of African-American speech but also of the black community's jokes, stories, music, and church sermons.

Langston's work influenced both blacks and whites, including black writers in Africa and the Caribbean, encouraging them to look to their own speech, music, and history as sources for their writing. He did not win major awards during his lifetime, but in the 21st century his work is finally gaining the recognition it deserves.

In addition to poems, Langston also wrote plays, musicals, newspaper columns, short stories, novels, and an autobiography. His strength was his ability to put important ideas and strong emotions into words that ordinary people could understand.

from "Theme for English B"

by Langston Hughes

I guess being colored doesn't make me NOT like

the same things other folks like who are other races.

So will my page be colored that I write?

Being me, it will not be white.

But it will be

a part of you, instructor.

You are white—

yet a part of me, as I am a part of you.

That's American.

Sometimes perhaps you don't want to be a part of me.

Nor do I often want to be a part of you.

But we are, that's true!

As I learn from you,

I guess you learn from me—

although you're older—and white—

and somewhat more free.

This is my page for English B.

Langston's first commitment was to the African-American community, but it was important to him that his writing reach out to all readers. He saw his writing as a way to fight against injustice, especially the injustices that black people faced every day. That could best be done if he spoke to people of all races.

In one of Langston's most widely published poems, "Theme for English B," he writes about a white teacher who asks his black student to write an essay about himself. The teacher tells the student to let the essay come out of himself so that it would "be true."

Throughout his life, Langston struggled to be true and to let his writing come out of his own experiences. He wanted his poems to express his experience as an African American as well as the experiences of the African-American community in general. He also wanted his poems to be weapons in the African-American struggle for full equality.

Langston Hughes was a writer of many different types of works. In his 65-year lifetime, he wrote poems, plays, short stories, and novels.

Chapter 1:
An American Beginning

Langston Hughes was born in Joplin, Missouri, in 1902. His mother and father separated when Langston was a baby, and his father moved to Mexico. Langston's mother was unable to support her son and left him with his grandmother in Lawrence, Kansas, while she worked in Topeka, Kansas.

Living with His Grandmother

Langston's grandmother read the Bible aloud to him and told him stories about his family and about slaves who struggled to be free. One of the stories she told him was about his grandfather, who died beside John Brown, an antislavery activist, in a battle to free the slaves. This story helped Langston form his sense of who he was and the ways a person could change the world.

As an adult, Langston said he had been an unhappy and lonely child. His grandmother was strict and spent most of her time

John Brown was an activist who gave his life to help free African Americans from slavery in the United States.

worrying about how to put food on the table. But he discovered books, and reading kept him from feeling quite so lonely. In the books Langston read, good conquered evil and poor boys like him always triumphed in the end.

Living with Auntie Reed

When Langston was twelve, his grandmother died and he went to live with Auntie Reed, a family friend, outside Lawrence. His mother was living in Lincoln, Illinois, and still could not earn enough money to keep him with her.

While Langston lived with Auntie Reed, he worked to help support the family. At a hotel near his school, he cleaned toilets, hallways, and the lobby. He was paid fifty cents a week. Langston used some of his money to go to the movies. This led to one of his early experiences of racial **discrimination.**

In the deep South at the time, laws kept blacks and whites separated in public. But in Kansas, the owners of restaurants, hotels, movie theaters, and other places could choose whether or not to serve African Americans. One day, when he went to the movie theater, he saw a sign saying that they no longer allowed black people in.

Living with His Mother

When he was thirteen, Langston moved to Lincoln, Illinois, to live with his mother. She had remarried, and she and her new husband made enough money to have Langston live with them. The marriage also brought Langston a younger stepbrother.

At his new school, Langston was elected the class poet. This surprised him, since he had never written a poem. Even so, he wrote one for graduation, about how great his teachers, school, and classmates were. When he read it aloud, the crowd applauded loudly and he began, for the first time, to think of himself as a poet.

Young poets often use the poetry of older, more experienced poets as models for the writing that they do. Carl Sandburg, pictured here in 1919, wrote poetry that did the same kinds of things that Hughes wanted to do with his.

Cleveland

When Langston was ready to start high school, he and his family moved to Cleveland. There Langston discovered the poems of Carl Sandburg, and they affected him deeply. Sandburg wrote about everyday life and ordinary working people—something very few poets did at that time.

Sandburg became one of the most important influences on Langston's work. He helped Langston see that poetry could be about his own life, not just about grand themes.

In a Poet's Words

"I was very unhappy and lonesome, living with my grandmother. Then it was that books began to happen to me, and I began to believe in nothing but books and the wonderful world in books."
—Speaking about how books helped him with loneliness early in his life

"So my first poem was about the longest poem I ever wrote—sixteen verses, which were later cut down. So at graduation, when I read the poem, naturally everybody applauded loudly. That was the way I began to write poetry."
—Speaking about how he got started writing poetry

"Now it was just sunset, and we crossed the Mississippi, slowly over a long bridge. . . . I began to think what that river, the old Mississippi, had meant to Negroes in the past. . . . Then I began to think about other rivers in our past—the Congo, and the Niger, and the Nile in Africa—and the thought came to me: "I've known rivers," and I put it down on the back of an envelope I had in my pocket."
—Speaking of how he wrote his famous poem, "The Negro Speaks of Rivers"

On his second visit to Mexico to see his father, Hughes, pictured here in 1922, wrote one of his most famous poems, "The Negro Speaks of Rivers." He was still a teenager when he wrote it.

Chapter 2:
The Young Poet Finds His Voice

In 1920, when Langston was eighteen, he went to Mexico to stay with his father for the summer. His father had a big ranch there, and was making money, but Langston and his father did not get along very well.

Later, Langston said that summer was one of the worst times of his life. Langston's father told him that he had moved to Mexico because there was less **prejudice** against African Americans there, so he could make more money than he could in the United States.

But as much as Langston's father didn't like people being prejudiced about him, Langston felt his father was prejudiced against Mexicans. Langston was uncomfortable with his father's constant complaints about Mexicans. He learned Spanish and became close to many of the people who worked for his father. Langston also learned that summer that his father was not proud of being African American, and this was another cause of tension between them.

College Decision

In September, Langston returned to Cleveland for his last year of high school. He became an editor of his high school yearbook, and he kept writing poetry. He was elected class poet again, and by the time he graduated he had filled a notebook with his poems.

After he graduated, Langston's father wrote and asked him to come back to Mexico. He offered to pay for college if Langston wanted to go. Langston didn't want to spend any more time with his father, but did want to go to college, so he felt he had to go to Mexico.

"The Negro Speaks of Rivers"

Langston was on the train, heading toward Mexico, when he looked out the window and saw the Mississippi River. It was sunset, and the train was crossing the river. Langston began to think about other rivers that were important to African-American history: the Niger, the Congo, the Nile. On the back of an envelope, he wrote a poem that would later become famous, "The Negro Speaks of Rivers."

"The Negro Speaks of Rivers" sketches a thousand or more years of African-American history. It describes African-American history as the flow of many rivers, both in Africa and in the United States. It was one of the first pieces of African-American

This train is riding along bluffs on the Mississippi River. It was a view like this that inspired Langston to write his famous poem, "The Negro Speaks of Rivers."

from "The Negro Speaks of Rivers"

By Langston Hughes

My soul has grown deep like the rivers.

I bathed in the Euphrates when dawns were young.
I built my hut near the Congo and it lulled me to sleep.
I looked upon the Nile and raised the pyramids above it.
I heard the singing of the Mississippi when Abe Lincoln
       went down to New Orleans, and I've seen its muddy
       bosom turn all golden in the sunset.

I've known rivers.
Ancient dusky rivers.

My soul has grown deep like the rivers.

writing to celebrate the greatness of African history, just as Europeans had for so long celebrated European history. For centuries, everything African had been dismissed as primitive and barbaric. What Langston saw, though, was depth and beauty.

Columbia University

In Mexico, Langston and his father argued about where he should go to college. Langston wanted to go to Columbia University, where he thought he could study literature and become a writer. He chose Columbia in part because it was near Harlem, an African-American section of New York City. His father wanted him to study engineering in Switzerland.

Langston's father asked whether writers made any money, and whether there were any African-American writers. Langston told him that some writers did make money from their writing, and that there were well-known black writers, in Europe as well as in the United States. They finally compromised. Langston's father agreed to Columbia University if Langston would study engineering instead of literature.

In 1921, Langston moved to New York and enrolled at Columbia, but he was unhappy there. The school felt too big, and he was not interested in engineering. Instead of studying, Langston read books and went to the lectures that interested him. He attended plays and shows. At the end of the year, Langston quit school. He wrote his father and told him not to send any more money.

His Own Man

At this time, very few jobs were open to African Americans, and those jobs paid less than jobs that were open to whites.

Langston found work for the winter as a mess boy, a kind of kitchen helper, on a ship docked in the New York harbor. Even though the boat wasn't sailing anywhere, he enjoyed working with the sailors. He loved talking with them and hearing their stories about faraway places.

During this time, he wrote one of his most famous poems, "The Weary Blues." In it, he tried to create in poetry the rhythm and sound of the blues. Blues music grew out of the songs that had been sung by African-American slaves, and it was now popular with people of all races.

In the spring, Langston took a different job as a mess boy. His new ship, the S.S. *Malone*, was sailing for Africa. As it left New York Harbor, he took a box of his old engineering and math books and threw them overboard. He vowed to be his own man from then on.

This is what the south part of Harlem, a neighborhood in New York City, looked like during the time when Hughes moved there to attend Columbia.

Many writers travel to see the world and experience new things. Langston was one such writer. He put the things he saw and did on his travels into some of his writings.

Chapter 3:
A Man of the World

Langston traveled up and down the west coast of Africa on the S.S. *Malone*. He saw both the Niger and the Congo Rivers, which he'd written about in "The Negro Speaks of Rivers."

Langston loved being in Africa, the land of his ancestors, but it hurt him to find that Africans didn't think of him as an African. Because he had mixed ancestry, his skin was lighter than theirs and his hair was straighter.

Africa was the only place in the world where he had been called a white man. That made him realize that even though Africans and African Americans were linked, their histories were different and their cultures were different.

Paris

Langston's next job was working in the kitchen of a freighter going between New York and Rotterdam, Holland. He sailed the English Channel and the North Sea, surviving strong winds and rough seas.

After a particularly rough trip, he quit his job when the ship docked in Rotterdam, and took a train to Paris. Paris was considered the center of the art world and was home to many African-American artists, who did not face the prejudice there that they faced at home.

Langston had dreamed of seeing Paris. He was 22, and he arrived in Paris broke, having spent all his money to get there.

Dr. Alain Locke

Langston found work, first as a doorman at one nightclub, then as a waiter at another. There, he met artists of all kinds, including many African-American blues and jazz musicians. Like the blues, jazz grew out of the African-American culture. Although some whites in the United States dismissed jazz and blues as primitive, in Europe they were greeted as one of the most important forces shaping modern culture.

While in Paris, Langston also met the visiting African-American philosopher and scholar Dr. Alain Locke, who later played an important role in the **Harlem Renaissance.** Dr. Locke

This painted portrait of Dr. Alain Locke hangs in the Smithsonian Institution in Washington, D.C.

This photo of the little St. Marco Square in Venice, Italy, was taken around the time that Langston was visiting the city.

read Langston's poetry and was impressed by its celebration of African-American life and by its use of blues rhythms. He asked for some of Langston's poems and published them in his magazine, *Survey Graphic*.

The nightclub where he was working closed, and Langston was out of a job. He took a train to Venice, Italy to meet Dr. Locke, who showed him the great museums and landmarks there.

Dr. Alain Locke

Dr. Alain Locke was one of the most important intellectual leaders of African-American history. He was one of the founders of a movement of artists and intellectuals that would become known as the **Harlem Renaissance,** or the "New Negro Renaissance." This movement, mainly of artists, musicians, and writers, developed during the late 1920s in Harlem, a neighborhood of New York City that was mostly black.

Locke believed that African Americans were capable of great literature and art. But at the time, African Americans in the arts did not receive the attention they deserved, due to racism. In his famous essay, "The New Negro," Locke wrote about the importance of black art, music, and culture to all of society.

To support his essay, Locke compiled literature and poetry from some of the best and brightest African-American writers of the time. A few of these artists included W.E.B. DuBois, Zora Neale Hurston, and Langston Hughes. Locke's article was widely read by members of both the black and the white communities.

Passage Home

When he left Venice, Langston meant to travel back to Paris by train, but his money and passport were stolen. To get home, he tried to get a job aboard a ship, but many ships wouldn't hire African Americans.

Langston finally found a ship with an all-black crew. The captain let him work as a steward in exchange for a ride home to the Unites States. He wasn't paid for his work, but he was homesick and was relieved to be heading home.

Langston had learned a lot from his travels. His time in Europe had shown him that blacks were not **discriminated** against everywhere in the world.

Like many African-American artists in Paris, Langston found that the French were able to see him as an ordinary person, not so different from themselves. This seldom happened in America at the time, and it helped him imagine this same kind of freedom at home.

This ocean liner is the kind of ship Langston would have sailed and worked on as he went from the United States to Africa and Europe.

This is the office and staff of the NAACP's Crisis *magazine, in which some of Langston's poetry was published. The man standing on the right is W.E.B. DuBois, one of the well-known figures of the Harlem Renaissance.*

Chapter 4:
The Poet Speaks of Rivers

Some of Langston's poetry had been published in magazines in the United States even before he arrived home. One poem, "Brothers," was published in *Crisis* magazine, and this brought him to the attention of African-American readers across the country.

Crisis was published by the **National Association for the Advancement of Colored People (NAACP),** and it was the most important national black magazine of the time. "Brothers" spoke of the bond linking black people who lived all around the world.

Seventh Street

Poetry didn't bring in enough money to pay the bills. Langston's mother had separated from his stepfather, and she and his stepbrother needed his support. In November 1924, Langston moved in with them in Washington, D.C. Although Langston loved

This is a view down Pennsylvania Avenue in Washington, D.C., during the mid to late 1920s—the time when Langston lived there.

Duke Ellington (on the right, playing the piano) was a famous musician who lived in Washington, D.C., at the same time as Hughes and his mother. By the time this photo was taken in 1943, both Ellington and Hughes had become famous for their art.

his mother and helped support her throughout her life, he was an adult now, and used to living on his own. It was hard for him to move back in with her.

But he loved the black community in Washington, D.C., and spent a lot of time hanging out on Seventh Street, in the heart of the community. He loved the sound of black people's voices, their laughter, their music. He loved the blues, but he also loved church

Before he became a famous poet, Hughes took various odd jobs, such as waiting tables, to earn a living. Here he is working as a busboy.

music and the way people danced when they felt the spirit of the Lord upon them. In his poetry, he tried to capture the sights, sounds, and spirit of the people he knew on Seventh Street.

Discovered

To pay the bills, Langston took a job as a busboy at the Wardman Park Hotel. One day, he recognized a famous white poet, Vachel Lindsay, eating in the dining room.

Langston had gained some recognition as a poet by that time, but he wanted to know if this famous poet thought his writing was as good as he hoped it was. He may also have hoped that Lindsay would help promote his career. Langston handed Lindsay three poems, explained that they were his own, and said he liked Lindsay's work. Before Lindsay could say anything, Langston turned and walked away.

Lindsay's response was generous. He read Langston's poems at a public performance that night, and praised him. He also sent Langston some books of poetry and wrote him, encouraging him to keep writing. "Hide and write and study and think," he advised.

The next day, the local newspaper carried an article about the "Negro busboy poet" Lindsay had discovered. When Langston came

from "The Weary Blues"

by Langston Hughes

In a deep song voice with a melancholy tone
I heard that Negro sing, that old piano moan—
    "Ain't got nobody in all this world,
    Ain't got nobody but ma self.
    I's gwine to quit ma frownin'
    And put ma troubles on the shelf."

Thump, thump, thump, went his foot on the floor.
He played a few chords then he sang some more—
    "I got the Weary Blues
    And I can't be satisfied.
    Got the Weary Blues
    And can't be satisfied—
    I ain't happy no mo'
    And I wish that I had died."
And far into the night he crooned that tune.
The stars went out and so did the moon.
The singer stopped playing and went to bed
While the Weary Blues echoed through his head.
He slept like a rock or a man that's dead.

to work that morning, reporters were waiting for him. They interviewed him and took his picture holding a tray of dishes in the dining room.

The story and the picture appeared all over the country. Suddenly Langston was known all over the United States as a poet. Diners at the hotel often asked to see the "busboy poet." They embarrassed him. And it was hard to "hide, write, study, and think." Soon he quit his job at the hotel and found another, cooking in a fish and oyster house.

A Prize-Winning Poet

In 1925, his poem "The Weary Blues" won a prize of $40 from *Opportunity,* the magazine of the **National Urban League.** This was his first literary prize.

That same year, he won a second literary prize, from *Crisis* magazine, and in 1926 he published his first book of poems, *The Weary Blues.* In 1926, he also got a scholarship to attend Lincoln University, near Philadelphia. The scholarship gave him a chance to study literature—the subject his father would not let him study at Columbia—which was what Langston had wanted to study all along. He took every American and English literature course that was offered, getting As in all of them.

Langston poses with a sculpture created by an African-American artist during the "New Negro Renaissance," or Harlem Renaissance.

Chapter 5: Harlem Renaissance's Man of Letters

After Langston graduated from Lincoln, he moved to Harlem. Harlem was then known as the center of black America, and Langston was one of many African-American artists, musicians, writers, and scholars living and working there.

The African Americans in Harlem were creating work inspired by African-American history and experience, and their belief in the importance of what they were doing brought a powerful sense of excitement to the community. This time came to be called the **Harlem Renaissance,** after a period of similar cultural growth in Europe centuries before.

Pride in the Black Community

This was an important time for Langston. He was discussing writing and politics with other African-American artists who, like him, celebrated the African-American community. He gained from knowing them and from knowing that they respected his work.

Langston's writing was well known now, and reading it helped make many African Americans proud of their history and heritage. It was also read by many readers who were not black, and it helped them appreciate that African-American artists were an important part of American art and culture—something that was not widely understood at the time.

The Great Depression

In 1929, the United States entered the **Great Depression.** These were tough economic times, and it became harder than usual for artists and writers to support themselves. The community of artists who had formed the **Harlem Renaissance** drifted apart.

Times were hard for everyone, not just for artists. All around him, Langston saw people losing their jobs and being put out of their homes because they could not pay the rent. Many people went hungry. He became interested not just in equality for African Americans but also in economic justice.

Langston continued to write, and in 1930 he published a novel, *Not Without Laughter*, based on his boyhood in Kansas. It won the Harmon Gold Award for Literature, an important prize recognizing African-American achievements.

A doorman stands in front of the Cotton Club in Harlem. Many famous African-American jazz musicians played here during the Harlem Renaissance.

Meeting Jim Crow

In 1931, Langston went on a reading tour of the southern United States. He felt especially honored to read his poetry at the Hampton Institute in Virginia, where Booker T. Washington had gone to school. More than a thousand students and faculty members attended the reading.

Booker T. Washington was a famous African-American leader who lived during the late 1800s and early 1900s. He had grown up as a slave and was freed after the Civil War. He believed getting an education was the most important thing African Americans could do to improve their lives, and he started a school that helped freed slaves learn job skills so they could support themselves.

Langston's tour through the South brought him into contact with a more extreme form of **segregation** than he had experienced in Kansas. For example, if a white person and a black person met on the sidewalk in the deep South, the black person was expected to step off the sidewalk until the white person passed. African Americans could not look white people in the eye—they were supposed to look at the ground instead. Laws called **Jim Crow laws** kept African Americans from using the same hospitals, waiting rooms, or restaurants as whites, or from using public restrooms or drinking fountains that were reserved for whites only.

Langston was often the victim of segregation on this tour, and it disturbed and angered him. More and more of his poems were about the unfair treatment of African Americans.

Socialism's Influence

Langston became increasingly convinced that **socialism** could bring economic justice to ordinary working people. Under socialism, property such as factories and businesses are owned by the public instead of by individuals. In 1932, he traveled to Russia to see for himself what socialism was like there.

Booker T. Washington, seen here in 1908, did not live to hear Langston Hughes read his poems at Hampton Institute. Washington died in 1915 after a short life of 59 years.

Langston later said that his three weeks in Russia gave him a realistic look at socialism. He saw many problems there. People weren't free to criticize the government, and instead of sharing the wealth equally, some people had much more than others.

He also found that many Russian people had mistaken ideas about the United States. They expected all white Americans to be rich and drive big cars and thought all African Americans lived on plantations and were uneducated. He spent a lot of time trying to explain what the United States was really like.

Even though Russia turned out not to be the model he had hoped for, he continued to believe that something needed to be done to change economic and political injustices around the world.

A Full-Time Writer

When he returned to the United States, Langston settled down in Carmel, California, where a friend offered him a small cabin by the ocean. There he wrote for eight to twelve hours every day, completing one or two magazine articles or short stories a week. From this writing, he made enough to support himself and his mother, who was in poor health.

Langston's father died in 1934, and Langston went to Mexico for his funeral. Their relationship had not grown any easier over the years, and Langston struggled to put the bad feelings he still carried about his father to rest.

That same year, Langston's play *Mulatto* was produced in New York. The word mulatto means a person who is part black and part white, and the play was about a young man with a white father

This is the Kremlin, a government building in Moscow, Russia's capitol city. This photo was taken between 1930 and 1934, around the time when Langston was visiting.

and a black mother. It was set in the deep South and dealt with the racial conflicts of its black and white characters. Langston was not happy with some of the changes the director made in his play, but it was well received and ran for a year on Broadway. The play then toured for two years.

Langston kept writing, as well as speaking and reading to audiences, no matter what his critics said about his work or beliefs.

Chapter 6:
Poetry, Race, and Politics

Although many people liked Langston's work, he had his critics. Some white readers felt threatened by his celebration of black culture and saw him as a troublemaker, stirring up bad feelings between the races.

In 1940, a national magazine, the *Saturday Evening Post*, published a poem of Langston's that he did not want in print. He had written it years before, and it no longer represented his thinking. The poem made fun of people who preached Christianity but would not put it into practice when they dealt with African Americans. It also suggested that Russian-style **socialism** might be a way for African Americans to gain their **civil rights.**

The poem caused Langston a lot of trouble. His critics accused him of hating the United States, and even though he tried to explain that this was not true, he lost a lot of public support and it became difficult for him to publish his writing.

Hughes found ways to earn a living from his writing. This is unusual for any writer, but especially for an African-American poet during the time of segregation.

Still, many people felt he was being unfairly treated and came to his defense, and they gave him the strength to get through this difficult time. A bishop of the African Methodist Episcopal Church, who was very critical of the poem at first, later said that the attacks on Langston were narrow minded. Slowly the tide began to turn in Langston's favor. The criticism died down and he was able to publish his work again.

Through it all, Langston continued to write and to give lectures and readings. He began work on a collection of poetry, *Shakespeare in Harlem*, which he told a friend was "lighter in tone—but not too light."

Writing in Wartime

The United States entered World War II in 1941. Having experienced **discrimination** himself, Langston saw the Nazis' hatred of Jews as a great evil that had to be defeated. The Dutch Underground, a secret organization fighting Nazi occupation of the Netherlands, secretly published a small book of Langston's poems. They saw that their struggle for freedom was not so different from his, and they drew strength from his work.

In the United States, Langston wrote jingles and slogans for the Treasury Department, helping to sell defense bonds. In some of his poems, he linked the fight against Hitler to the fight against discrimination in the United States. In "How About It, Dixie," he wrote, "Look like by now / Folks ought to know / It's hard to beat Hitler / Protecting **Jim Crow**."

In 1941, an all-black theater company in Chicago, the Good Shepherd Community Players, produced another of Langston's plays, *The Sun Do Move*. This was a musical about the **Underground Railroad,** a group of antislavery activists who helped slaves escape from the South before the Civil War. Although the group couldn't bring Langston's play to as big an audience as a Broadway production would, it was important because the play was put on by an African-American theater group. This meant that African Americans could make the artistic decisions involved.

Taking a Stand

In 1942, Langston published *Shakespeare in Harlem*. It was his first major collection of poetry in fifteen years. The poems touched on the struggles, joys, triumphs, and trials of Harlem's African-American residents.

The next year, he published the first of his stories about Jess B. Semple, whose nickname was "Simple." He continued to write Simple stories for the next 23 years. Simple was based on a real man Langston had often met and talked with in Harlem—an average, hard-working African American.

The Simple stories always began with Langston meeting Simple at a neighborhood bar. Simple would talk about current events, both at home and around the world. He would comment on **civil rights** and the problems facing African Americans. His views were often insightful and always humorous. The stories appeared in African-American newspapers across the country and were much loved by black readers, who saw in them their own daily conversations and views.

Langston wrote poems about everyday people, like this woman in Harlem in 1943.

Langston continued to lecture and go on reading tours, speaking at high schools, colleges, and universities around the country. He talked to both black and white students about the importance of African-American history. He also spoke out against the racial **discrimination** that African Americans faced. One of his hopes was that he could help promote a better understanding among people from different racial, religious, and cultural backgrounds.

Accused of Communism

In 1953, Langston was called before a Senate committee investigating the influence of **communists** in the United States. Communists here wanted to introduce a socialist system similar to the one Russia had at the time, and at the time many people in the United States felt they were a threat to the country.

Many of the people who were called before this committee were falsely accused of being communists and enemies of the country. But even though the accusations were false, they lost their reputations, their jobs, and sometimes their friends. When Langston appeared before the committee, he was asked about his political beliefs and activities. He explained that he no longer held the same views he had held as a young man. He said he had never been an enemy of the country and was not a communist.

Unfortunately, that wasn't enough. Langston's reputation suffered as a result of his appearance and he lost many speaking jobs. When he did give lectures and readings, he was often picketed. In the African-American community, however, Langston was still well respected, and he kept on writing. In the years after his committee appearance, he wrote an average of two books a year, including children's books and collections of his Simple stories.

Hughes answers questions and defends himself before members of a U.S. Senate committee in 1953.

Already a distinguished poet when this picture was taken in 1958, Hughes, 56 years old at the time, had no idea how much his work would influence African-American artists who had yet to be born.

Chapter 7: Returning to the River's Source

During the 1950s, Langston wrote more **prose** than poetry. Some of his work was translated into Spanish and influenced poets throughout Latin America. As it always had been, the central subject of his writing was freedom.

The Dean of Negro Writers

By the early 1960s, Langston was known as the dean of Negro writers. However, some critics dismissed him because his writing was simple and easy to understand. But his work had depth in its feeling and its understanding of life, and beauty in its sound and rhythm.

Langston's work influenced many younger black writers, including the poet Gwendolyn Brooks and the playwright Lorraine Hansberry. He was generous in giving his time to young writers. He often helped them publish their work, and he wrote back to those who wrote to him, offering encouragement and advice. "Do not be afraid of yourselves," he advised young African-American writers. "You are the world."

Langston didn't want to see African-American writers limited to writing about racial issues. In 1965, when he began to write a regular column for the *New York Post,* he wrote about issues of interest to all readers as well as the racial issues facing the country. But he always saw himself as a black writer, not "just a writer."

A Poet Dies

Langston died suddenly, on May 22, 1967, from complications of what he had thought would be minor surgery. The news surprised his many friends. The Cuban poet Nicolás Guillén wrote, "The truth is that I could expect anything from Langston except the fact that he might die." At the funeral, someone read one of Langston's poems:

> Tell all my mourners
> To mourn in red—
> Cause there ain't no sense
> In my bein' dead.

At one time in his life, Langston had asked that an old jazz tune be played at his funeral, to make his friends laugh. Its title was "Do Nothing Till You Hear from Me."

Today people all over the world know and admire the writing of Langston Hughes. His poetry, with its use of jazz, blues, slang, everyday speech, and church sermons, helped the writers who

Rap music carried on Hughes's tradition of using everyday forms of speech to create art that celebrates African-American culture. Run-DMC, pictured here in 1987, were pioneers of this music, and were among the first rap groups to become popular.

followed him imagine new ways to write about their experiences. Even rap music, which began long after Langston's death, owes him a debt for helping poets appreciate the power of the rhythms and slang they heard on the street.

Langston was also important because he helped change old ideas about race in the United States. His poetry, plays, novels, short stories, magazine articles, and autobiographies were weapons

Langston Hughes became so famous and well known after he died that people began to name schools and other institutions after him. The teacher here is teaching algebra at the Langston Hughes Elementary School in Chicago.

in the fight for equality. They gave a public voice to a group of people who had been despised or ignored by Americans of other races, and they showed the depth and richness of black culture. In this way, his writing has had a lasting effect not only on literature, but on society as well.

from "Night Funeral in Harlem"

by Langston Hughes

When it was all over
And the lid shut on his head
and the organ had done played
and the last prayers been said
and six pallbearers
Carried him out for dead
And off down Lenox Avenue
That long black hearse done sped,

    The street light
    At his corner
    Shined just like a tear—

That boy that they was mournin'
Was so dear, so dear
To them folks that brought the flowers,
To that girl who paid the preacher man—
It was all their tears that made

    That poor boy's
    Funeral grand.

    Night funeral
    In Harlem.

Glossary

civil rights   personal freedoms that are guaranteed to all U.S. citizens

communists   people who wanted to introduce a system of government like Russia had during most of the 1900s

discrimination   singling something or someone out, often unfairly, because of some feature they possess

Great Depression   period of time lasting from 1929 through 1939, when millions of Americans lost their jobs

Harlem Renaissance   period of time during the 1920s when African-American arts and culture flourished in this neighborhood in New York City. It was also known as the New Negro Renaissance.

Jim Crow laws   system of laws imposed in the South that separated African Americans from whites in all areas of public life

National Urban League   African-American organization to help blacks deal with economic and social discrimination

National Association for the Advancement of Colored People (NAACP)   national organization formed to seek civil rights for African Americans

prejudice   negative attitude toward others, often based on race or religion

prose   writing that is not poetry

segregation   keeping different groups, especially people of different races, separate

socialism   system of government that favors the needs of the community as a whole over the needs of the individual

Underground Railroad   secret organization that helped slaves escape to freedom before the Civil War

Timeline

1902: Langston Hughes is born in Joplin, Missouri, and spends his early years living with his grandmother in Lawrence, Kansas.

1909: Hughes' grandmother dies. He lives with family friend Auntie B.

1915: He moves to Lincoln, Illinois, to live with his mother. Writes his first poem after being elected class poet.

1916: Moves to Cleveland, Ohio.

1919: Wins *Opportunity* award for "The Weary Blues."

1920: Graduates from Central High School in Cleveland. Goes to Mexico and lives with his father for a year.

1921: Enrolls at Columbia University in New York. Majors in engineering but drops out after one year.

1926: First book of poems, *The Weary Blues*, is published.

1929: Completes his college education at Lincoln University in Pennsylvania

1930: First novel, *Not Without Laughter,* is published.

1932: First children's book of poetry, *The Dream Keeper*, is published.

1934: Collection of short stories, *The Ways of White Folks,* is published.

1935: His play *Mulatto* opens on Broadway.

1940: Autobiography, *The Big Sea*, is published.

1950: First humor collection, *Simple Speaks His Mind* is published. It features columns about the character Jess B. Semple.

1953: Testifies before a Senate committe investigating **Communism.**

1967: Dies on May 22, 1967, in New York City.

Further Information

Further reading

Hill, Christine M. *Langston Hughes: Poet of the Harlem Renaissance.* Berkeley Heights, N.J.: Enslow Publishers, 1997.

Osofsky, Audrey. *Free to Dream: The Making of a Poet, Langston Hughes.* New York: HarperCollins, 1996.

Walker, Alice. *Langston Hughes: American Poet.* New York: HarperCollins, 2001.

Addresses

National Association for the Advancement of Colored People
4805 Mount Hope Drive
Baltimore, MD 21215

The National Urban League
120 Wall Street
New York, NY 10005

Institute for African American Studies
312 Holmes
Hunter Academic Building
University of Georgia
Athens, GA 30602

The Academy of American Poets
588 Broadway
Suite 604
New York, NY 10012-3210

Index